Fast Track
Learning
(English)

OLANREWAJU AKINFENWA

DEDICATION

This book is dedicated first to the honour of God, the Giver of Life! Thereafter, to all who desire to improve their lives and refused to be stagnant.

CONTENTS

ACKNOWLEDGMENTS

This book is dedicated first to the honour of God.
Thereafter, I must thank my wife, Mrs. Yetunde
Akinfenwa for her support. There are numerous other
people that contributed to this work of learning but I must
mentioned few due to space. These are: Mrs. Grace
Adekunle, Proprietress of Flourishing Schools for her
encouragement. Mr. Remi Ayanlade, Proprietor of Cypress
International Academy for his encouragement. Pastor and
Mrs. Ajani of the Graphael Publishing Company, Mrs.
Damilola Ivan-job for reading through, Mrs. Comfort
Olaosun for reading through and Mrs. Bibitayo Salman for
reading the manuscript.
Any error found in the work is solely mine.

1 ALPHABETS AND WORDS

Big letter alphabets:

A B C D E F G H I J K L M N O P Q R S T U V W X Y Z

Small letter alphabets

a b c d e f g h i j k l m n o p q r s t u v w x y z

The alphabets contain 26 letters and one, two, three, four, five and more letters are combined to form words.

It is divided into two main groups called vowels and consonants. There are five vowels and twenty one consonants.

Vowels

A, E, I O, U

Consonants

B,C,D,F,G,H,J,K,L,M,N,P,Q,R,S,T,V,W, X,Y,Z

As much as it is important to know this structure, we will not dwell on it for now. We will move straight to the use of these letters to form words and see how they are used in day to day activities.

Examples:

A, is a letter and can be a one letter word as in "I am a boy".

In the above sentence two letters: "a" and "I" served as words.

Letters "a" and "m" were combined above to form a two letter word "am"

While letters "b", "o", and "y" were combined to form a three letter word "boy"

Two-letter words

A+n = an;

A+m = am

Three-letter words

a+n+d = and

B+o+y = boy

B+u+y = buy

Four-letter words

G+o+o+d = Good

F+a+i+r = Fair

P+a+s+s = Pass

F+a+i+l = Fail

Five-letter words

D+a+n+c+e = Dance

Q+u+e+e+n = Queen

F+r+a+i+l = Frail

V+e+r+v+e = Verve

F+l+i+n+g = Fling

Exercises

Write 5 two-letter words starting with letter "A"

e.g.: A + { n } = An

A + {   } =

A + {   } =

A + {   } =

A + {   } =

A + {   } =

Write 5 three-letter words starting with letter "B"

e.g.: B + {o} + {y} = Boy

B + {   } + {   } =

B + {   } + {   } =

B + {   } + {   } =

B + {   } + {   } =

B + {   } + {   } =

Write 5 four-letter words

e.g.: {C} + {A} + {R} + {T} = CART

{   } + {   } + {   } + {   } =

{ } + { } + { } + { } =

{ } + { } + { } + { } =

{ } + { } + { } + { } =

{ } + { } + { } + { } =

Write 5 five-letter words

e.g.: {A} + {P} + {P} + {L} + {E} = APPLE

{ } + { } + { } + { } + { } =

{ } + { } + { } + { } + { } =

{ } + { } + { } + { } + { } =

{ } + { } + { } + { } + { } =

{ } + { } + { } + { } + { } =

Write 5 six-letter words

e.g.: {L} + {E} + {T} + {T} + {E} + {R} =
LETTER

{ } + { } + { } + { } + { } + { } =

{ } + { } + { } + { } + { } + { } =

{ } + { } + { } + { } + { } + { } =

{ } + { } + { } + { } + { } + { } =

{ } + { } + { } + { } + { } + { } =

Read out:

At, rat, cat, bat, mat, sat, fat, cart, mart, fart

Boy,   boil,   ball,   box,

2 FORMING SENTENCES

Sentences are formed with words. Like we have in letters, there are also one-word, two-word, three-word sentences, etc.

There are Simple Sentence, Complex Sentence, Compound Sentence and Compound-Complex Sentence

One word
I, am, a, boy, who, loves, eating, pizza

Two words

I am, he is, she is, they are, we are

Three words

I love eating, she loves cooking, we love partying

Four words

I am a boy, she is a girl, we are a family

A Boy

I am a boy.

I am putting on a shirt and a short.

On my shoulder is a bag.

I am putting on a socks and a shoe.

A belt is used to hold my short.

A girl

I am a girl

I am putting on a gown.

There are pleats on my gown.

I am putting on a shoe.

My hair is plaited.

Sentence – alphabets recognition with introduction to numbers

The quick brown fox jumps over a lazy dog.

This is a sentence that contains all the alphabets.

It has letter **a** standing alone and in l**a**zy

Letter **b** is in **b**rown

Letter **c** hides in qui**c**k

Letter **d** starts the word **d**og

Letter **e** ends th**e** and it is the third letter in ov**e**r

Letter **f** is the first letter in **f**ox

Letter **g** ends the word do**g**

Letter **h** is in the middle of t**h**e

Letter **i** is in the middle of qu**i**ck

Letter **j** is for **j**umps as **a** is for **a**pple

Letter **k** ends the word quic**k**

Letter **l** is for lazy as **h** is for

hardworking

Letter **m** is in ju**m**ps

Letter **n** ends brow**n**

Letter **o** stands in between **d** and **g** to form d**o**g and is also found in br**o**wn and f**o**x as well as in **o**ver

Letter **p** is in jum**p**s

Letter **q** starts the word **q**uick

Letter **r** is the second letter in b**r**own and the fourth letter in ove**r**

Letter **s** is the fifth letter in jump**s**

Letter **t** is the first letter in **t**he

Letter **u** is the second letter in quick as well as j**u**mps

Letter **v** is also a second letter but not in words, quick and jumps but in the word o**v**er

Letter **w** is the fourth letter in bro**w**n

Letter **x** is the third and the last letter in

fo**x**

Letter **y** is the fourth and the last letter in

laz**y**

Letter **z** is the third important letter in

la**z**y

How many letter words are the following

from the sentence alphabets recognition

above?

e.g. Standing = (8)

Hides = ( )

Starts = ( )

Ends = ( )

Third = ( )

First = ( )

Middle = ( )

Stands = ( )

Between = ( )

Found = ( )

Second = ( )

Fourth = ( )

Fifth = ( )

But = ( )

Last = ( )

Important = ( )

Assignment

From the above Sentence Alphabets recognition passage explain the following words:

Hides =

....

....

Starts =

....

....

Ends =

....

....

Third   =

....

....

First   =

....

....

Middle   =

....

....

Stands   =

....

....

Between   =

....

....

Found   =

....

....

Second =

....

....

Fourth =

....

....

Fifth =

....

....

But =

....

....

Last =

....

....

Important:

....

....

3 WORDS REVISION AND
INTRODUCTION TO NUMBERS

We are starting this chapter with a puzzle to remind us of what we learnt in the last chapters.

TAHBECQDUEIFCGKHBIRJOKWLNMFMOOXPJQURMSPTSUOVVWEXRYAZLAZYDOG
TAHBECQDUEIFCGKHBIRJOKWLNMFMOOXPJQURMSPTSUOVVWEXRYAZLAZYDOG
TAHBECQDUEIFCGKHBIRJOKWLNMFMOOXPJQURMSPTSUOVVWEXRYAZLAZYDOG
TAHBECQDUEIFCGKHBIRJOKWLNMFMOOXPJQURMSPTSUOVVWEXRYAZLAZYDOG
TAHBECQDUEIFCGKHBIRJOKWLNMFMOOXPJQURMSPTSUOVVWEXRYAZLAZYDOG
TAHBECQDUEIFCGKHBIRJOKWLNMFMOOXPJQURMSPTSUOVVWEXRYAZLAZYDOG
TAHBECQDUEIFCGKHBIRJOKWLNMFMOOXPJQURMSPTSUOVVWEXRYAZLAZYDOG
TAHBECQDUEIFCGKHBIRJOKWLNMFMOOXPJQURMSPTSUOVVWEXRYAZLAZYDOG
TAHBECQDUEIFCGKHBIRJOKWLNMFMOOXPJQURMSPTSUOVVWEXRYAZLAZYDOG
TAHBECQDUEIFCGKHBIRJOKWLNMFMOOXPJQURMSPTSUOVVWEXRYAZLAZYDOG
TAHBECQDUEIFCGKHBIRJOKWLNMFMOOXPJQURMSPTSUOVVWEXRYAZLAZYDOG
TAHBECQDUEIFCGKHBIRJOKWLNMFMOOXPJQURMSPTSUOVVWEXRYAZLAZYDOG
TAHBECQDUEIFCGKHBIRJOKWLNMFMOOXPJQURMSPTSUOVVWEXRYAZLAZYDOG
TAHBECQDUEIFCGKHBIRJOKWLNMFMOOXPJQURMSPTSUOVVWEXRYAZLAZYDOG

Circle out 2, 3 4, 5, 6 and 7 letter words from the puzzle. Your circle can be diagonal, front or back circle as in the examples shown.

Introduction to Numbers

There are only ten figures we use as numbers.

These are: 0,1,2,3,4,5,6,7,8,9

Zero, one, two, three, four, five, six, seven, eight, nine

We join one or two or three or more to form other numbers.

Examples; 1 and 0 is 10 (ten)

1 and 1 is 11(eleven)

1   2 3 4 5 6 7 8 9 10
11 12 13 14 15 16 17 18 19 20

21 22 23 24 25 26 27 28 29 30

Complete the number to one hundred

First, second, third, fourth, fifth, sixth, seventh, eighth, ninth, tenth.
Read aloud with the teacher leading to the one hundredth.

Roman figures

i   ii   iii   iv   v   vi   vii   viii   ix
x
xi   xii   xiii   xiv   xv   xvi   xvii   xviii   xix
xx
xxi xxii   xxiii xxiv xxv xxvi xxvii xxviii xxix
xxx

Complete the roman figure to one hundred

Exercise

Write the names of animals that you know and state how many letter word that they are.

For example:

Hen is a three-letter word = (3)

= ( )

= ( )

= ( )

= ( )

= ( )

Write the names of parts of human beings that you know and state how many letter word that they are.

For Example:

Shoulder is an eight-letter word = (8)

= ( )

Fast Track Learning (English)

= (   )
= (   )
= (   )
= (   )

4 SENTENCE CONSTRUCTIONS

A sentence is a set of words that is complete in itself. It usually contains a subject and predicate.

A sentence can convey a statement, question, exclamation, or command, and can have a main clause and sometimes one or more subordinate clauses.

Conversation

Conversation between two friends

Ade: Good morning Sayo

Sayo: Good morning Ade, how is the family?

Ade: We are good and you?

Sayo: We are also good.

Ade: Where are you going to this early morning?

Sayo: I am off to my workshop.

Ade: This early morning? Hope there is no problem?

Sayo: I need to complete a set of chair a customer will be picking up by 9:00 am

Ade: Okay, that is good. I wish you safe trip.

Sayo: Thanks and I wish you a great day.

Sayo left and Ade called out to a hawker

Ade: Hello, what are you selling?

Hawker: It is plantain sir.

Ade: Come over. Good morning, how much is a bunch?

Hawker: It is N600 per bunch sir.

Ade: Can I pay N400?

Hawker: If you pay N550, I will sell it to you sir.

Ade: It is too early for us to be bargaining, let me pay N450.

Hawker: Okay sir, pick your choice.

Usage of words

Words can be used for a unit (singular) or for many (plural). There are regular plural or complex plural. For the regular plural, you need to add only "s" to the word to form its plural whereas for the complex, a word ending with "y" may take regular "s" ending as in "boy – boys" and "ies" in "baby – babies".

Singular	Plural
Boy	Boys
Man	Men
Girl	Girls
Woman	Women
Baby	Babies
House	Houses
Room	Rooms

Some words are gender specific, especially pronouns. That is, some words are used only for male while others are used for female. For us to understand this we need to learn some words and their opposites.

Word	Opposite
Woman	Man
Girl	Boy
Mother	Father
Mistress	Master
Literate	Illiterate
Good	bad
Noise	silence

Greetings

In greetings there are specific words for male and for female as you will see in the examples below:

Good morning

This is used in the morning.

To greet a **man**: Good morning **sir**

To greet a **woman**: Good morning **ma**

The greeting form for man is "sir" and for a woman is "ma". You cannot say "Good morning ma" for a man. That would be wrong.

Good afternoon

This greeting is for afternoon period.

To greet a **man**: Good afternoon **sir**

To greet a **woman**: Good afternoon **ma**.

Good evening

This is for the evening period

To greet a **man**: Good evening **sir**

To greet a **woman**: Good evening **ma**.

Good night

This is used when one is calling it a day. That is when one is closing or leaving one's acquaintance or colleagues and there is the possibility that you will only get to see each other the following day.

To greet a **man**: Good night **sir**.

To greet a **woman**: Good night **ma**.

The word "sir" is associated with the male gender while "ma" is used for the female gender as you will notice in the below conversation. Pay attention also to the pronouns used for the two genders and the neuter gender.

Conversation

Master: Good morning class

Class: Good morning sir (chorus)

Master: Soji, how are you this morning?

Soji: I am fine **sir**.

Master: Did you eat before coming to school?

Soji: Yes **sir**. I ate before coming to school.

Master: What did you eat?

Soji: I ate beans

Master: Ajitoni, what is the name for the food Soji ate in the morning?

Ajitoni: **It** is called breakfast

Master: Good, clap for **her**.

The whole class clapped for her.

Master: Isiaka, what is the food we eat in the afternoon called?

Isiaka: Afternoon food is called lunch sir.

Master: Correct, clap for **him**

The whole class clapped for him

Master: Oluwaseun what is the food we eat in the evening?

Oluwaseun: It is called dinner sir.

Master: Correct, clap for **him**

The whole class clapped for him.

Master: Aregbe what is the food we eat at midday called?

Aregbe: It is called midday meal sir.

Master: No! That is wrong. Who can answer the question?

Oluwaseun and Amina raised their hands.

Master: Oluwaseun, you have answered a question, let Amina take a shot at this.

Amina: It is called brunch sir.

Master: Clap for **her**.

The whole class clapped for her.

Note: The neuter gender pronoun "it" could be seen representing the noun "breakfast", "lunch", "dinner". For example it would not be appealing if the noun is repeated often and often. To solve this, pronoun takes its place.

E.g. "The breakfast I took was pap, the breakfast was hot and the breakfast scalded my tongue".

Though the above could be said to be correct but the real correct way of writing or speaking English Language is to use pronouns in some places instead of the actual noun.

E.g. "The breakfast **I** took was pap, **it** was hot and **it** scalded **my** tongue".

The neuter gender pronoun "it" was used twice to represent "breakfast" and it makes the sentence flow.

New words

Breakfast, brunch, lunch, dinner, he, she, it, clap, tongue, twice.

5 INTRODUCTIONS TO ENGLISH GRAMMAR

Part of Speech

Noun, pronoun, verb, adverb, adjective, preposition, conjunction and interjection

Noun

Noun is a name of a person, animal, place or things.

For example: **Ade** is the owner of the **dog** that trashed the cushion **chair** in the **church**.

The "noun" words in the sentence are in bold

Types of noun

There are different types of noun. These are: Common noun, Proper noun, Concrete noun, Abstract noun, Collective nouns, Countable and Uncountable noun

Exercise

List five "noun" words to show that you understand the definition of a noun.

Pronoun

Pronoun is a word used in place of a noun

Ade is the owner of the dog that trashed the cushion chair in the church. **He** apologised on **its** behalf to the vicar **who** was furious. **His** mother stormed the church and reprimanded **him** while **she** also pleaded with the vicar **who** had visibly calmed down. **He** warned Ade to always put **his** dog on leash.

The "pronoun" words in the sentence are in bold.

Types of pronoun

There are various types of pronoun. These are:

1. Personal Pronouns

2. Object Pronouns

3. Possessive Pronouns

4. Reflexive Pronouns

5. Intensive Pronouns

6. Indefinite Pronouns

7. Demonstrative Pronouns

8. Interrogative Pronouns

9. Relative Pronouns

10. Archaic Pronouns

Exercise

Identify the "pronoun" words in the passage and state who they represent:

Ade is the owner of the dog that trashed the cushion chair in the church. He apologised on its behalf to the vicar who was furious. His mother stormed the church and reprimanded him while she also pleaded with the vicar who had visibly calmed down. He warned Ade to always put his dog on leash.

Verb

Verb is a word that describes action of a subject or state or who a subject is and forming the main part of a predicate.

For example:

Action: Ade **dances** every evening. The verb "dance" states Ade's action.

State: Ade is **kind**. The verb "kind" states who Ade is.

Types of verb

Action Verbs
1. Transitive verbs

2. Intransitive verbs

No-Action Verbs
1. To be verbs

2. Linking verbs

3. Auxiliary verbs

Verbs form

There are two main types of verbs. These are regular verbs and irregular verbs.

The regular verbs could be conjugated into five main parts:

Infinitive, Present Tense, Past Tense, Past Participle, Present Participle

For example:

The regular verb "to be" can be conjugated as follows:

Form To Be	
Infinitive:	be
Present Tense:	am
This can be further conjugated to third person singular:	is
and third person plural:	are

Past Tense

(Singular):	was
(Plural):	were
Past Participle:	been
Present Participle:	being

Irregular verbs

Irregular verbs unlike the regular verbs do not end with "ed" if conjugated to past tense.

For example a regular verb "play" has its past tense as "played" but an irregular verb "begin" has its past tense as "began".

Adverb

An adverb is a word that changes, modifies or qualifies words like adjective, a verb, a clause, another adverb, or any other type of word or phrase.

Types of adverb

Adverb modified the verb in how an action takes place, how often an action takes place, where an action takes place and when an action takes place.

This gave rise to the four types of adverb.

Manner: Easily, loudly, soundly, etc

Place: Top, inside, near, etc

Time: Now, soon, tomorrow, etc

Frequency: Daily, frequently, sometimes, etc

For example:

Manner: I jumped over the bar easily.

The girl was snoring loudly.

The girl slept soundly.

Place: My copy of Fast Track Learning is at the top of the box.

He is hiding inside.

She lives near Toun's house.

Time: Come here now.

He will arrive soon.

We will travel tomorrow.

Frequency: You must brush your teeth daily.

Shola visits me frequently.

We met sometimes ago.

Adjective

Adjective is a word that describes or clarifies a noun or pronoun. It makes a noun or a pronoun more understandable.

Types of adjectives

Descriptive, Quantitative, Demonstrative, Possessive, Interrogative, Distributive, Articles.

We will not go into the nitty-gritty of this but let us just demonstrate how adjectives modify words.

For example:
In our sentence formation example we had the sentence: "**The quick brown** fox jumps over the **lazy** dog". The adjectives are in bold.

Exercise:
In our earlier conversation, we found out that Ade, Soji and Ajitoni were brilliant students while Aregbe was a dullard.

Underline all the adjectives in the sentence.

Preposition

Preposition is a word that indicates the relationship between a noun and the other words of a sentence. It explains relationships of sequence, space, and logic between the object of the sentence and the rest of the sentence. A preposition helps us understand order, time connections, and positions.

Example:

I am going **to** Ede.

Ade threw a stick **at** the dog.

My mother locked my trinkets **inside** the box.

My parents have gone **out** of town.

Types of Preposition

There are five different types of prepositions. These are: Simple prepositions, Double prepositions, Compound prepositions, Participle prepositions and Phrase prepositions

Examples of prepositions:

Under, above, to, in, off, by, since

Exercise:

Write seven sentences using one or more of the above prepositions.

Conjunction

Conjunction is a joiner, an uninflected linguistic form that joins together sentences, clauses, phrases, or words.

Examples are: "and" , "but", and "although".

Types of conjunction

There are three major types of conjunctions. These are Coordinating Conjunction, Subordinating Conjunction, Correlative Conjunction.

Interjection

Interjection is a word or phrase that is grammatically independent from the words around it, and mainly expresses feeling or emotion rather than meaning.

Types of interjections

- Interjections for Greeting - Hello! , Hey! , Hi!
- Interjections for Joy - Hurrah! , Hurray!, My o my!, Boy o boy!
- Interjections for Approval - Bravo! , Brilliant!, Great!
- Interjections for Surprise - Ha! , Hey! , What!
- Interjections for Grief/Pain - Alas! , Ah!, Goodness! Oh no!

Punctuation

Punctuation is used in writing to separate sentences and their elements and to clarify their meaning.

The sentences below explain how punctuation can be used to change, separate and clarify meanings.

A man without her woman is nothing.
A man, without her, woman is nothing.
A man, without her woman, is nothing.

Types of punctuation

Full stop (period), comma, semicolon, colon, exclamation, question mark, dash, quotation marks, brackets, hyphen, braces, ellipsis, parentheses and apostrophe

Full stop (Period): (.) This punctuation is used to denote the end of a sentence. It is one of the three punctuations that end a statement or sentence. The other two are: Question mark and Exclamation mark.

Comma: (,) is a mark of punctuation that is used to indicate a division, a pause, a phrase of clause. There are grammatical rules guiding the use of comma as a punctuation mark, but the easiest rule is to note when an idea is ending, when a division between a sentence occurs especially when it is followed by a slight pause or when different items are within a sentence and there is a need to itemise each and differentiate them without listing them out in numbers.

Comma is also used when there is a need to write large figures like one thousand – 1, 000, one million – 1, 000, 000.

Comma is so important and it can change the meaning of a sentence from what it is intended.

Example:
Let us look at our earlier example to

note and bring home the importance of the comma as a punctuation mark.

A man without her woman is nothing.

A man, without her, woman is nothing.

A man, without her woman, is nothing.

Semi colon: (;) is used to separate major elements in a sentence. A semicolon can be used between two closely related independent clauses, that is not already joined by a coordinating conjunction. Semicolons can also be used in place of commas to separate items in a list, especially when there are other usages of comma in the sentence.

Colon: (:) used to precede a list of items, a quotation, or an expansion or explanation. It is also used to separate time format e.g. 1:30 pm.

Exclamation: (!) Exclamation mark is used to express high or strong feelings or to show emphasis, express exasperation, surprise or to end a sharp phrase. It can be called emotion punctuation.

Question mark: (?) is a punctuation mark that indicates a asking sentence, that is, a question or an interrogative clause or phrase.

Dash: (—) is a long horizontal bar, much longer than a hyphen. It is used to separate two ideas, in between a sentence to explain a preceding idea.

Quotation marks: (" ") (informally known as quotes and speech marks) are used in pairs. The first is the opening quotation mark while the second is the closing quotation mark. It is used when another person's speech or idea is introduced in a paragraph. It is also used to mark an unusual word, a phrase or a quotation.

ABOUT THE AUTHOR

Olanrewaju Akinfenwa is a trained journalist with a degree in Book Publishing. A member of the Nigerian Union of Journalist, NUJ, a Member of Chartered Institute of Bankers of Nigeria and a Fellow of Certified Institute of Cooperatives and Social Enterprise.

An astute entrepreneur, he is into farming and food processing.

He is married with children

CPSIA information can be obtained
at www.ICGtesting.com
Printed in the USA
LVHW050032040323
740875LV00003B/347